THE Cool AND Warmth OF Hearts

J.A. SANTANA

DOWNLOAD THE FREE AUDIOBOOKS!

Grab your <u>FREE</u> audiobooks of
Shadows Amongst the Threads and
The Cool and Warmth of Hearts, narrated by me!

Experience the chilling world of fear and the
passionate realm of love in a whole new way.

JASANTANA.ME/SHADOWSHEARTSAUDIO

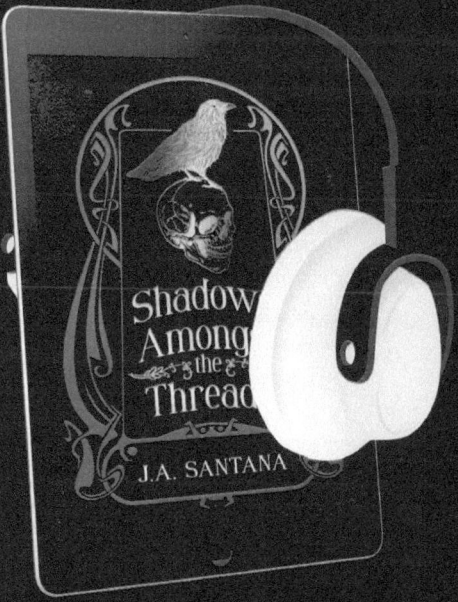

paperback ISBN: 979-8-9854620-1-2
hardcover ISBN: 979-8-9854620-2-9
e-book ISBN: 979-8-9854620-0-5

Library of Congress Control Number: 2021925400

Cover & Typeset Design: *Natalia Junqueira*
Editor: *Nicole Fegan*

*To my family and friends,
and Lady Muse*

CONTENTS

EPIGRAPH

The vices of love are the scorching flames of the sun and the chilling frost of the poles; and the virtue of both is the basking warmth of sunrays and the cooling breeze of zephyr.

—J.A. Santana

INTRODUCTION

This poetry collection of romantic love poems shares a history as far back as Mesopotamia with *The Love Song of Shu-Sin* and *The Song of Solomon* in the Old Testament of the Bible. In Classical Greece and Rome where traces of it are found in Greek Tragedies or Ovid's *Metamorphoses* and his love poems. And even into the early Renaissance of Dante Alighieri's secret love for Beatrice and his epic poem *The Divine Comedy*; and later with William Shakespeare's plays and sonnets, and then onto Romanticism featuring Lord Byron with his Byronic hero and magnum opus *Don Juan*; the notion of love still permeates to this day. When the inception of love and romanticism was a primitive yet lingering force in my earlier years and with the passage of time, I've grown a fondness and comprehension of it—yet it still eludes me; and one where commonfolk, artists, poets, authors, psychologists, and philosophers surmise the concept of love never changes, but how we talk about it does. With that said, I want to provide context and intention behind this collection. You will recognize several things about it: the length of poems, section themes, and narrative arc of both arrangement and individual poems. Most of these poems align themselves as narratives but not tread too much as prose; where the story is at the heart and it's in our nature to sprinkle enough commitment to wander in these landscapes. Each section is organized by their primary theme: pining, being in love, heartbreak, love of life, and power of love; in addition, the prologue and epilogue poems opens and close the collection with a romanticized cosmic sensibility of love that isn't just a concept but a universal one we can explore and in between are varied perspectives that hits close to home. Although poetry is the art of compression in saying a few chosen words; I believe the balance of telling a story about love while respecting the varied forms, style, rhythm, and musicality of language in these poems—pays homage to the harmony in a poetry collection that will offer some solace in your dealings with love. This collection is an inspiration—not just my experiences, but also those I observed secondhand or mulled over philosophically. As you read these verses of sense and sentiment that encompass the complex beauty of human nature with its contention to love; I hope you can find a piece in here that shares your compassion with it.

Prologue

The Cool and Warmth of Hearts

Paradise, once a lush haven of flora and fauna
and the sin of human,
met in midsummer;
then, a winter breeze blew into next summer
to hide the sin and shame
in death that followed and once held
the love of life its fame.

Entrapped in an iceberg,
astonished to find frozen hearts
pacified and alone,
and with time will atone;
desolate frigid barrens
persisted for eons, then
a gentle warm breeze
blew a kiss against the frosty ice-sheet lips
and melted the ice-rock,
where it laid a piece of entity,
not quite understood in the chasm of history.

The moment stood in a gaze
and simmered for days;
volcanic plumes shone
altered landscapes,
bursting from a body
enmeshed in a confetti of light.
It blotted the end of stilled nights,
strewn across the vast space where it did not delay.
Many cultures ascribed a deity
depicting a hearth where it mildly shone
a cool warmth as two figures cast a dance
in their own shadows,
gifting humanity fire to grant life its chance.

Pining

A Constant Remedy I

When in sight, utterance in her words is constant;
in its language, it petrifies and entangles a weary heart,
preemptive of the radiance in her smile.
I wander off in an amative thought—is love
legitimate and concrete as proclaimed by the Greats?
Or am I foolish to characterize her unusually unique traits?
I don't know where to start and search in my soul
to unearth a desire that burns to know—
have I transcended the gates of heaven?
But I lament in cold trembles, labeled *fornicator*;
to be seen upon by my Creator as a *malefactor*.

Thus, I delve deep into my emotions,
strew across several oceans
and seek counsel from the Greats:
Donne,
what have I done to deserve this reverie for this fair maiden?
Shakespeare,
what iambic pentameter verse would offer relief?
Byron,
is there a way we may find to cast away the skeleton's plea?
Dante,
why is it we endure in silence in our forte
and wish she understand the aim of our court,
as our consort?

Perhaps, I must subdue and sacrifice my intentions
and give rein to love's admiration—
where I bid her farewell and adore from my keep,
while I ruminate over past transgressions
and occasion the glow felt in her lofty ascension.

I shudder to think with a smirk as I lay
and cast a creeping fog
that fills the background to chant–
blood for blood,
element with element;
etched in these death throes
I hope to discover a remedy.

A Constant Remedy II

Lily had returned, an aura constant as light,
an aroma petrifying an unruly knight
whose rusted armor once struck
and scattered light in a dream
that wandered off in an amative thought
and sought counsel from heroes of pastime I hold in esteem:
Odysseus,
I fear Lily will honor suitors' attempts unlike Penelope;
Aeneas,
I wish not by the intervention of forces to sway me away
from Lily, as she may inflict a misery as Dido upon a pyre;
King Arthur,
torn between the affair of Kingdom
and Guinevere's waning affection,
your duty led to the downfall between all dominions.
Uncertainty persists in the remote hero's pastime
and from this wisdom I'll scale
heaven to save me one last time.

A bond that once aired with prestige,
but could not hold insincerely
for a soul, burning an undying yearn
that rattled the gates of heaven to give Word
of a cursed sinner stood before his Creator,
a swelling void in his weary heart,
who saw the glimmer in those threads ripping him apart
while chained to rock until a dreadful flood does impart
and lay his promises in tainted blood—departing
Hope from his shackles, he blossoms
from his rosebud to undo him from Lily's bosom.

A Renewed Feeling

A moment of despair I did not face
when a love so rare has such grace.
I scan daydreams unlike what my eyes
have seen of what belies
before the Athenian goddess
unfolds, before Adonis's modest
fate pines for his lady's divine tears.
Had we not enough time to fear?
How long have we gone to deprive
ourselves of a fruitful gift? Alive
by the prospect, a wedge in my rift
was spared a worse fate than guilt,
forgiving with a kiss that's swift.
Was our love not born and built
by melody sung to spawn forth
the sunrise? I witness its birth
pass the cracks of my window blinds;
awash in warm, vibrant light that finds
both ends of cheeks raised in delight.
Let spoils be given from a heartfelt place;
let the enticements not spare the space
of bonds shrouded before the onset.
Nature makes us agonize,
a longing that burdens us in debt.
But open arms, they hold what spies
and unfold the charms that tie
and cherish our memories bound
to immortal spirits that never perish.
Whispers fill her ear with devious dreams
not meant to devalue what seem
the quality of her worth. Found,
a rejected child who stood dejected,
only to shrink and shirk in his

former shadow and
Heaven divine him lady grace,
eager to share this very place;
a life devoid of displeasure and strife;
how much praise must I implore?
To hold steady hands and amble
through the vineyard and preamble—
a tale when the devil's tempt did bore
to express fated consequence,
bestow me with your presence;
did it ever prepare me, my dear?
The torture much grander, I fear,
did indulge what was near
of heart; frozen, did veer.
The light of dawn has spoken;
why I have fallen by love's token,
and fallen by the sins of this bind
did conscript a benign nature, only to find
the mercy you have shown did mind
to help atone for my sins to prove I have grown in kind.

A New Form of Being

A visage unseen in two years prior,
something swells and alights the fire;
enclosed in this classroom,
I can't help but embrace
every thought that lately looms
through my mind to retrace.
What has changed in our junior year?
Concerned by the proximity,
stirs a restless anxiety,
and this day enamored
by a cat-eye glance confined in this room;
the equanimity of this epiphany.
In this passage of time,
conveyed: plump lips covered in gloss,
adjacent to my right—
it was evident in your actions;
the slow fall lashes carried
by the weight of a smile,
adjacent to my right—
I bravely took the leap to encroach
upon where this may lead
as you instilled this feeling in me.
From this event,
a change of heart
over changing seasons;
two years before,
passing busy shadows,
and here I am dreaming.
Yet, you have been dreaming
many times before—
is that not treason?
Let it be known
that I wonder in a fantasy

what it's like to run my palms down your shoulders
and watch the invisible hairs perk up in response;
am I exceeding my capacity
for a fine lady I barely know?
I need closure to know
if I descend to the reach of your hands,
would I spark another renaissance?
I curl over your hands
and a sudden gasp of breath
pulls to resist until
you grasp it was me
and anchor your mind at ease.
An inborn stormy pleasure fills a well of desire
and claims my prize and calms the incessant fire.
Fine lady, you have awakened a nostalgic mystery:
Once thought lost in history,
I mused with a gaze adjacent to my right,
a lovestruck daze flushed me to do what's right,
and you sit there in solemn patience
while I'm wrapped by the imagination—
perched on the hilltop tree
over the grand pasture,
who could have foreseen
the love of this rapture?
I'm meticulously plotting to enrapture
you with unyielding passion to impress upon you
an overwhelming degree of enchantments,
a spectacle the gods of Athens have not seen the likes of
bear witness a soul who fashions a lover's request,
a refreshment that evokes sensations belligerent to the sense
and implodes a welt of desires,
foolish enough to be felt by troubled admirers.

A Ray of Sunshine

A ray of sunshine beams from you.
Words inscribed in your name,
  symbols etched in your name,
I am filled with joy with just the mention of you.
When the clouds won't part, it leaves a sting in my heart;
I cannot hold back now,
  just fold my thoughts into one vow
  and express them to you.
Hoping to make an impression before it's too late
or the shadow will continue at this rate.
Which of my crimes would be in the fate of God?
Don't want to end up as another passerby
under the gloomy sky.

I haven't been enchanted enough
to indulge in the spoils of life;
rather,
I'm struck by the gargoyles of strife.
How candid can I be in the shout of my plea?
I hold up a knife,
steep into the sky
with one request;
I can feel the thump in my chest
on this day
to pierce the veil
with the sacrifice of blood and find its way,
a memory of you that won't go away.
Instead of lingering
behind the opaque sky,
I'm calling out
for a ray of light
before the opaque sky
invites the blight;
I'll wait a lifetime to espy with my own eyes

the passing of rain.
Nothing more to say,
all for the same reason:
to impart today
with a little sunshine.
If I must trek all four seasons
in the same pair of shoes,
then so be it.
So long as you fulfill your part,
so be wise, reign
in, add a little shine
before the night comes.
And the winter is long
for I'm falling in love with a little sunshine;
for I'm falling in love with a little sunshine.
Before the day comes undone
and the winter is long
for a ray of sunshine.

Adonis & Venus

Patiently waiting from the cloud of my perch
     made my heart impatient,
the torment from this event has bent and writhed
     my soul complacent.
Can no mortal have an abstract thought of me,
when all of me has never taken earthly shape?
And here I hope for you to feel drawn to me;
     every time I glance,
you alter the hue of blue skies that drapes
the clues to impose my divine nature onto thee.

Stubborn as a dam to make no glance
     of the hues of passion that espy,
I had to find novel ways to reel the sheen from your eyes.
The more and more I saw with the eye,
the more and more it entranced my mind.
A stoic-manner fixated with his hounds
helped me visualize a story book of us and found
no pictures inside for us to find.

If it were a fantasy,
a drunken stupor awakes with a bottle of Hennessy,
find themself, and say, "Did I dream within a dream?"
A dream that builds upon my self-esteem—
what encouragement might make us a team;
     whilst,
I still hide behind this tree and wonder if my poetry
has the charm to alarm and press his throat to notice me.

Still in his placid gaze locked on his trophy,
and lost in my own and off to dreamland, I depart.
Pass between and shift his gaze on the figure of mine;
     struck by my sheer beauty,
his eyes swell at the figure of the divine.
Then he summoned his horse and saddled me behind
and galloped off to resume his hunt
and I embraced him ever more tightly.

An ear-piercing scream snapped me back to reality;
disoriented, I scouted around to pinpoint his location.
    Pacified in my gape—oh no! The cruel reality
that bounds the fate of earthbound mortals
revealed to me the pain of flesh and it bled profusely
from the only wound of the boar's tusk. An immortal
like I could not understand
    the plight of men's fallible hurdles.
    I lunged at his side
    and the hounds made their chase of those bloody
tusk into the shadow among the myrtles.

Forbidden with my own hands,
    I needed to nourish his wounds
    with the blessing of Jove,
    who imparted me with a lightning rod
    to smite the dormant misery that bled in this grove.
But silence drowned out the once-vibrant lush of the forest
and those apple-green eyes lost their hue
    to the cloudy husk of death,
and my lover now lives in the barren underworld
    from my love in one last breath.

If no immortal love could ever intermingle,
    I'll decree henceforth
that love encompass doubt, fear, and sadness;
this cold, stiff, and pale body bare of a soul's blood mingles
with the flowers and tints the pale rose red as love's emptiness.

Bereft of this tragic scene, I'll wager with his soul
and tack him on the night sky in the constellation of Taurus.
In the twinkle of the star,
    he will first notice the limitless sparkle;
each breath he draws fills a foggy clime
and cements another continuous lonesome night
as he adores me with the touch of light
——————————————— for all time.

Desperately

Desperately weakened by the astral sweetness in her eye,
it took a toll on my life,
and by a strange resurrection
I'm given a second chance at life
by the magic gleamed in those lovely, lovely eyes.
She cleansed the strife hidden within,
and one day, she'll be my one and only wife;
so much so, the difference found in her aspect
is a mystery in those eyes came down from the sky.

I stare into those glamorous eyes;
a glistening sunlight speck hangs at the corner.
Calm waves vacillate, back and forth,
a purified moment, not a tremor,
enraptured by the wrinkle of her nose.
Adoring with scrutiny a favorable pleasure;
is this not happiness—who knows?

I rest my head on her cushioned bosom;
I sense a rise in a throbbing rhythm
echoing in my ears,
chords struck and a pleasant tune; I hear
what lingers here bristle my ears,
a breeze whizzing by as the instrument plays a fine tune
as it came near.

I wish to squeeze her into me,
unite as one amalgamation by the cliff-side sea,
but I find much more reassurance by the coast
and watch her glow like moonlight
on this favorable, favorable lucid night.

Met with a blow of that earlier breeze
as it ripples through her hair,
shimmering like crystals dancing in the air;

oh, what an elation to sit at her side.
The spectacle of this fairest fair,
I hope it won't ever subside.

She is mine—she is mine,
I'll never let go, unless it comes with a price…
Only for a time, I'll reclaim my prize.
I'm desperately enthralled by her sheer sexual paradise,
I'm desperate to shout it,
"I'm desperately in love with thine!"

Doesn't Hurt to Try

Long, long ago, shrouded in the obscure glen,
at first, I did not regard you then;
I had no clue if you spotted me from the tree.
Let me reimburse with this verse,
to tell a tale of how much inspiration
      you have instilled in me.

Whether nature misaligned the paint of her stroke,
   a turbulent wind
provoked me north; I denied its request,
     then the howl of many surround,
but it did not stop me from seeking what I could have found.
If only the incessant trees could stop fanning their leaves,
I would oblige and set forth in nature's plea.

I wandered lonely on the unbeaten path,
not a sound for a time but the occasional chirp;
I could not discern—clashes with a warble
in between the ruffling of grass and leaves
disappearing in the hiss of air; unveil a footpath,
the sound of something fair farther ahead,
I had finally found the untrodden path.

The sound grew louder the nearer I drew;
I knew neither fawn nor fauna could produce
the familiar melody from its lot.
There I stood as the shadow of a tree
and there she stood as the rays of the sun;
what tempted an ancient goddess to these parts,
far from where the olives grew,
I did not know, but there I knew
stood my sweetheart.

I'm a poet who still has much to learn:
Restrain the beast lying within that burns

and succumb to what this fantasy unfolds
in the instrument of words—
don't expect my love can be bought,
    and place in thought
        my love as another knot
which you tie and stash away in Hollow's vacant lot,
then expect to nurture as you would with famine crops
to safekeep the harvest as the agitated storm
may blow its fierce winds and scatter our hopes.

Nor do I want words to suffuse:
I'm bribing an evening to lay with you as my excuse;
I'm not denying the fact something boils within to let loose;
It's only natural, for a man's attraction he could not choose.

Without purpose, what reason
without a will to claim our freedom,
lest the shapeshift season rails against such freedom.
Without being headstrong to admit our wrongs and
without the advice, someday misfortunate will arrive,
envelop the glow, and seal away in the darkest parts;
I think you and I know
        when we will have to depart
into the sightless snow.

I jot down what I should have spoken
and discover in passing seasons
how much progress could mend a heart broken;
and did I ever ask in reason
if a repressed past is apt to love again?
      Love did not deign
to admit its shame, so with this love,
      we give reign
as we try just as hard, bit by bit,
to utter, "It doesn't hurt to try again…"

Emotions

I cannot find the right emotions to convey.
In a game of Scrabble, I jumble around words to no avail;
my mind tumbles and wavers in the blank ocean of castaways;
what delusions am I having? As I struggle to rail,
Lady Muse, please help conjure perfect phrases;
but the hypnotic glance in her eyes makes my heart sail
away—
to the shores of unkempt cages
and sheltered nights alone with empty pages;
yet, I reminisce about the sway of a pendulum.
As I scrawl a thousand words,
none yet can speak.
A yearning to embrace swells for weeks—
I reject!
Until I am persuaded,
what I share next captivates her the next word or two
and captures my heart she has raided.
Still can't find the right word or two
to have her fall in love with me—
is that a bit cruel?
She may have her own word or two,
waiting on me,
but I struggle to think of one in love's duel.
Question myself—am I capable?
I don't want to know the answer,
I suspect I'm playing a fool's game,
repent for a promise I have not kept.
Then it dawns on me!
Your smooth skin elevates to new heights,
your lip illuminates a nightless sky,
your eyes ascend my soul to heaven,
you capture every aspect of my being.
Ah yes!

These are the words
that I feel.
No pencil to jot it down, nor paper to compose in a symphony,
I must keep my hands warm.
But I languish to let you know:
Encrypted in these messages
are the emotions I was hoping to convey.

How Do I

My eyes caught this foreign anomaly;
an exotic treat turned my heart gleefully.
What can I claim when I'm at the mercy
of ancient systems that beget me?
The moment my senses are engrossed in her aspect,
butterflies swarm and ravish my entrails.

Call me a fool, but I would still avail.
How do I thrill a lofty angel
when I tremble in her glow of night,
when I stumble in her shine of day?

The essence of life shows me the heed of its warning to see—
If I could prick a bite of her time
before it sways and sinks at bedtime.
How do I say hello
when I just want to lay down
in the wee hours on the phone?
How do I say "Hello, beautiful,"
when my eyes don't match my juvenile words?
How do I hug her
when I may smother her with joy?
How do I get to keep her
when I am loath to lose her to a competent boy?
How do I meet her
when I break down in haste?
How do I keep her from tormenting me
when I am tempted to chase?
How do I get rid of these feelings
when it's her I crave to embrace?

When chance delivers, I'll offer with a kiss
and reel from the hips, locked in a death grip,
until no pulse gives—Mujer Bonita,

how do I finish this precious moment;
insisting, I will diminish this rare chance,
before I lament
the death of this romance?

Lovers' Lane

The day I first set eyes on her,
Cupid's arrow struck.
Lost in a daze, admiring the occasion,
tracing my fingers of her curvature;
then, painting with my brush,
passing each stroke in careless motions,
I did not want to set hand from brush.
She made a glance my way;
pretending I wouldn't match the same,
jitters rippled throughout,
then I caught her sly smirk
and spellbound by the twirl
as it echoed down her dress,
sending chills plunging
to knock me off my feet.
A tightening in my chest
when she uttered her first word
crippled my every movement and
every effort, composing my posture
from collapsing as she sauntered closer,
the thermostat rose—
on this blazing day,
it did not help to keep my cool.
The narrowing in her eyes,
matched by a dignified smile,
agitated within me a dormant feeling felt for miles;
with each stride,
a gust-like force
blasted me in my pacification.
I braced the ground with more effort,
yet not a break in her composure,
while I broke out in a profuse sweat.

Then, she stood a foot from me,
sparks flinging in a chaotic manner.
A change in my disposition
I took notice of this imposition
bore by her seductive manner;
I, a pensive young poet
met her with a gratuitous smile;
she conveyed in her subtlety
how to live a life that's worthwhile.
Our arms reached out,
sparks growing fiercer.
Palms met—
a massive ripple of force blasted outward,
temperature rose to a broiling point,
the air shimmered in circles,
crystalize hands clutched,
the elemental chaos
ceased in a deafening silence.
Pride and devotion filled our world;
we strolled off into the horizon,
leaving behind a mark
for all to follow
on lovers' lane.

Passionate Blessing

I could not stop for my angel; she swiftly swiped me.
Is she life's blessing or is this life's cruel lesson for me?
On this conflicted day, I find it quite strange—
heaven and hell
clashed at the gate!
An angel like her has shown me from her flight,
apocalypse further along from nigh.
I could not fathom fate
while enamored in her clutches tonight.

I could not grapple with the infighting,
nor did it matter, when I was poised
to surrender to the hymn of her voice;
although, a grisly scene came at the seams—
not a fill of earth's firmament by heaven's gleam
as Armageddon tore a rift
between two factions; ravished landscapes
sundered a continental drift
between anointer and sinner among this hellscape,
and she swiftly flew away from the home I knew,
and awestruck coveted neighbors, delusional from the truth,
cast away from my sight
as pebbles rested on the river of woes
and mountains came into view.

Stretches of towns of hedonists partook
in their hedonistic endeavors
and the monsters of below came to drag them
into the fiery pit of Lucifer's kingdom.
The gape of many pacified from our flyby
and, unperturbed of themselves, further and further
dragged into hell,
and not a damned soul lived to tell—
in sentences they could speak, but all were awry.

Enthralled by the passion of journey's aimless flight,
east we went and never quite north.
Then came the eve of twilight
and the rear displayed a spectacle of fireworks, henceforth
snuffing out the white
by the hue of an agitated face
and the gleam of an innocent face.
And nightfall poured on us with the sublunary theme
smiling back in the reflection of the lake's pristine,
meditative state and the fate
of this exchange from the mountain's overcast lay
in the woods which she occasioned for us to stay.

Time's unmerciful grim,
     saved by my beloved a misery of aeons;
humanity's existence persisted for eons upon eons,
and apocalypse gave birth to a familiar paradise;
    rose dawn at my angel's side
         stood a clime cover in rime
and roamed among the new Garden of Eden for all time.

Pleasure

A pleasure you desire lies inside a treasure;
it cannot measure by one's own frantic pleasure.

Quite a leisure to admire for the mind this night,
rising at the onset cushion against this pleasure.

You lurk upon my chest—the cost? Free of charge, and
this sacred night lingers throughout our life's pleasure.

A radiance grows—etched in this vision, won't die
in the tale of temptation who is called by name: pleasure.

An overwhelming presence lingers inside you;
caught in your gaze, amazed to jostle tonight's pleasure.

Reforms love and informs with shame, but loving you,
I have flourished from the nourishment of pleasure.

Always remember, never forget; what comes next?
Sturdy hands move closer in this heat of pleasure.

Gentle passes of lotion glide across the skin;
ah—silken sand, don't mistake the rites of pleasure.

I impressed a smile by the weaving of strokes with
these palms escalating the next stage in our pleasure.

A faulty gesture I have not committed, but
laid on the surf I saw bent and felt a sea of pleasure.

Space which distance marks that spans time and some more
unravels a pattern—particle of pleasure.

And I, *The Speaker*, capable of this dance,
am signing off—here I marked a memoir of pleasure.

Secret

I see you across the room.
My heart vigorously pounds
to the beat of a drum;
I hope it subsides before
it's too loud!

I want to tell you how I feel,
but I cannot;
I want to tell you how much I desire you,
but I cannot;
I want to tell you how I long for you,
but I cannot;
I want to tell you how much I need you,
but I cannot.

I want to tell you how in details—
the sensation you make me feel
reveals what this secret entails
which I no longer must conceal,
but you're not ready.
I want to feel your soft lips,
but you're not ready.
I want you to feel the goosebumps
that skip my heart in too many jumps,
but you're not ready.
I want to read you a line from this poem
before the sight of you fills my lips in foam,
but you're not ready.

A visceral feeling
deep inside craves
to let the world know—
you are my first love.
I feel hands stretching apart

both sides of my body,
I hear it already;
"What a fool!"
my Ego imparts,
and it befools my love
and now, I cannot let you know
that I know what I know;
yet, I wish that I could show
how I sever firmament betwixt heaven and earth
and shout the secret love I held shown its worth.
How did secrets ever cloak themselves,
when rifts gouged for miles,
left behind an image of a dazzling smile,
and this secret lays etched in these rocks dial?

Unravel

What could it be?
Am I a fool to hide from idyllic perfection;
and the heart does not see,
I'm not worthy of her affection?

What is it in my personality that rejects me from beauty?
In a sense, she projects the shape of a rare rose cruelty.

Do you hear the melody of poetry?
No, I don't mean the perfect rhymes;
remember when I jostled Jane to jump for joy in jest
and it sprung a smile on her face as love's test?
I suppose the source of this love is made blunt;
still, within the image of her lies a power one must confront;
what height must one climb to achieve her affection?
Am I tested by time to await my destiny as her affliction?

An hour has swept by;
I feel my insides being devoured by some untapped entity.

Maybe I'll regain my sense when she delivers her kiss—
what am I saying?
I'll fall into unconsciousness
just by the touch of her silk skin,
scorching my heart in inflammation;
I'm out of my mind to go to these lengths!
What am I still saying? Is this not madness?
Who does not want the tragedy of a woman's fixation?

I'm sorry for having all these mysteries;
she'll live a foundation in history,
before our bodies lie beneath the earth's gravel.
I'd rather play the fool's game
than be a coward who never unravels
his true aim...

In Love

A Fatal Kiss

A kiss like candy Swiss—in this moment of bliss,
time stretches infinitely, awaiting a battle of two sources
that rattles the cosmos with undue force—
an aroma escapes her pores, pours over
to sink my ship in the depths of the abyss
and renews a sense sometimes missed in a simple kiss.

As she descends onto the bed; reminisce,
how a kiss insists upon my lips.
I oblige to caress the silk of her skin, a delicate game of sin;
I worry my sandpaper palms might graze her delicate skin.

Devilish eyes swarm with the allure of spellbinding charm;
her sultry lips scream to tug me further in her binding;
my fingers clasp at the side of her hips in one last finding
to unwind me from her death binding.

The room boils over as hell's fury unleashes—
a second not to skip;
my heart throbs in a colossal burst of flames;
a warmth soars to my fingertips
and her eyes flare in a cosmic snap.
I clutch tighter with a tease;
all of me wants her so greatly
and with this closure I wrap
her with my love the onset ease.

I cease for a moment, a cat-and-mouse game—
we play to find a place that lurks within to bait
and assert in stoic-pride with fortune on my side.
She exhales a warm breeze and tingles

the invisible hairs on my ears;
I counter with much the same; yet,
a seductive, menacing glare
in the corner of her eye tears
a dull spot I cannot identify.

Tensions escalate to emerge:
a tidal wave one-hundred-feet high sweeping a city
a thousand times over,
a detonation clearing out the population
many times over,
a haughty hurricane toppling several homes,
an avalanche burying a town,
an earthquake tearing at the seams of a countryside,
a restraint driving me mad
the longer I drive her to wait at my side.

Aloof to my agonize-pain,
she devilishly smiles in silent prayer
to illuminate some clues to reveal the illusions
she played in this game...I failed to miss,
and then juxtaposed eyes meet to realize a fatal kiss.

Anticipating

Feeling blue, not quite in the mood;
can I piece together a clue that may lead me to you?
Always willing to support my needs—
I realize your thoughtful gestures
bring joy in these times of instability.
I'll cherish your benign and loving nature;
these are genuine values,
to model in our children, so long as we continue to nurture,
and the Matthew effect will only multiply in our favor.
My every fear and concern,
whisked away in the wind—
that's love's power
that has bloomed from this flower.
How the complaisance of such love
bridge the solemn patience of self-love.
I'll never forbid the memories,
how the warmth in your touches
balanced me.
Lonesome nights
have their share of doubts;
I wonder about your whereabouts
and it only left me with more doubts.
I must be insane to think this way
and this empty house has not felt the same
since you went away.
My love, return before the next night
takes its toll;
soon, let's take a stroll
in the Garden of Eve,
before the eternal unease
grows in our hearts.

A longing has lasted for hours,
it has been several weeks,
I'm terrified it'll soon be several months.
Please return before the hearth oxidizes;
I'm anticipating being at your side.

Be With You

When I hear her voice
over coffee chatter,
should it matter
if one's rejoice
should reminisce
of first lovers' kiss.
Birds chirping
on this morning,
I am met with a breeze cruising pass,
a tender touch as it rolls off the skin.
It did amass a tranquil moment,
and help utter a sigh of relief,
and I follow a leaf lifted by the song of her voice;
to be this close…
is all I need of this sin.
The scent of her skin
sends comforting ease; yet,
this peace will not last,
as sparks electrifies
and ripples throughout the body.
I sense a rise in pulse--beating swifter
and more pronounced with each fated encounter
nearing two bodies.
In her twinkle smile she pats my forearm
in elongated strokes,
which ends with a tranquil smile…yes,
that's all it would take, a tranquil smile
and a simple touch.
When I glance at her,
I survey an art Pablo Picasso
could not craft;

Nature has bested him
with millions of years
of perfecting the strokes of her brush.
Before me, she presents her masterpiece.
Examining the synchronicity in the way
she conveys gesture
by the utterance of her words,
I am mesmerized.
She puts on a dance—
inspires me to get up and take her hand,
twirling her around like a spinning top.
A sunny smile beams in all directions;
chuckling along to the festivity theme song—then
I clutch her in—to unfold in this embrace.
As the air grows still,
no other place
I'd rather be
but this one.
Nothing but her and me exist,
in this time
matched by a benign, petrifying glare
for all to admire it's her only crime.
Life often filled with scenes of quarrels,
but we are not immortal, so
let's take the time and scrutinize the art
surrounded in these laurels.
The scent of these laurels,
almost akin to her red lips coral;
I am possessed by this beloved scent
as it spreads to lay the animals to rest.
Sometimes a kiss should not be wrest,
a love so rare is this not blessed—
an upswing breeze,
circling and circling until
we are no longer seen.

No one saw,
not even the curious animals
nor the prying trees.
What a strange phenomenon,
oh—behold! An imprint on the ground
shows they went eastbound;
yet, they could not be found
and yet, there is not a sound
that bound these lovers.

Composition of Love I

A proposition inscribed in this letter:
"I alone appeal to you, for I,
once a nameless, shameless, and aimless vagrant,
drew a covenant; awaken with a name, shame, and aim
and do not heed the contract would center
bombastic criteria many would deny
and result in my ailing prison.

When I speak
the utterance of a word, I feel in my throat a knot
if it's not praising you.
When I breathe,
I only do when you have commanded, or I shall rot
and endure a wretched tightening in my chest,
growing more grotesque.
When I walk,
each hesitant step cripples and dismantles my knees,
if I am not traveling towards you.

If the image of you
does not reflect off my window,
I'm good as dead without a shadow.
If I stray, I will disperse as dust in the wind.
The narrow road ahead, lost in a mist, I will find
on this sightless departure the union of a kiss.
Horatio, how's one to imagine with their heart
and not with a lack of sense? Impart
where reason and intuition are in accordance,
to evoke a reality
that leads me to my singularity.

As old fools sayeth, 'Love is hate, hate is love.'
In either claim, no matter how vain,
once it's comprehended, it's no longer ordained
by the composition of our love."

Composition of Love II

A proposition inscribed in this second letter:
"If I astray,
 so will my heart stray
 in the barren gray husk of Kronos;
 while you wander into the narrow trail shrouded in mist…
 I hope an echo of you ripples through to mark with a kiss…
 Attend with your heart,
 not by what you see and hear;
 you're often misled, that's why we're invoked in fear.
 Love conjures up hate,
 hate urges love.
 It may sound insane, but once it's comprehended,
 it's no longer a strain in our lofty hearts…"

Composition of Love III

A proposition inscribed in this final letter:
"I hope this time, it echoes better.
Love, I alone appeal to you...once a
nameless, shameless, and aimless fool in our covenant.
When words sway,
I only revert to what we can measure in weight...
When I breathe,
I only do it despite this bizarre dream...
Wandering down this dusty road had dismembered my knees.
If I'm not destined to you...
What am I saying? Is this coming from me? What are these?
Vague images reflected off my stained window—
why does this burden bear me forth to these dead willows?
If I astray,
and I must stray,
a cliché one has to say—
in order to live another day
from your thrall; yet,
faint images of you stretching towards the mist...
I stand here too long for your kiss...
Then, a vibrant strand of you, how did I miss.
Bestowed in these phrases...
'Study with your heart,
not by what a fool can glean with his senses.
You're often misled, that's why we are invoked in fear
and often make messes,
as love and hate are interconnected.
It may sound vain, but these are the chains that held it.'"

Grateful

I'm grateful she has appeared in my life,
and the former, disappeared with my strife,
adored the traits that enhance her beauty,
with many aspects shone through her duties:
kindness in troves to inspire authors,
gathered to furnace the art in honor;
awaiting the gleam on their gleeful faces,
while light shimmers and bounds in her tresses;
sturdy like the turtle, steady by time,
sublime in the soul sang of her springtime.
How virtue invites the divine to us
and ceases the ravish inside of us;
how can I repay in equal amount?
Marriage suffices, in all lives will surmount.

I Love You

I'll still love you when the soil on Earth runs dry
and when the flowers on Earth wither away.
I'll still love you when my heart boils in the sultry
———————————————— summer of July
and the dour look in your eyes goes astray,
and when the broken column that once felt the sunlight glee
and the sea that once held the origin of life
and the vacant distant night sea
are only told of the billows and surfs of strife.

I love you more than
sky gave flight to Hermes's message;
I love you more than
mountains gave rise to Ragnarök's howl;
I love you more than
the sea surfaced Poseidon's wrath.

I love with a love
just as equal to the Lord from above;
I love with a love
just as evil as the hellish King beneath the sea;
I love with a love
just as fresh-born couples squabble their tales of love.
I love with a love
just as all the same as thee.

Like doves swarming the skies,
reaching new heights,
nosediving over adversity,
I must admit we're truly in love…

I Think I'm in Love

Love has struck with a tremendous shock.
I urge to purge this horrendous strain,
nibbling away every little bit
as ants crowd around my heart
to fortify a colony and drain
bit by bit
soul from heart.
I'm shattered like smashed glass
with no way to glue back the pieces,
disarrayed as the senses are.
Horrified like children are,
hearkening the creak in the attic,
how a bizarre thing could be so erratic.
What of this moment can ease my worries—
I floor it! Before this becomes the end of my story
but a tree reaches beneath the earth,
rooting my attempt as I try to evade.
I struggle to pull away,
and scattered oak brown seasonal leaves are in the way,
and the wind falls and whooshes me from the stubborn tree.
Sprinting alongside a river, I deprive what I chose
to ignore—
a blistering breeze dropped too many degrees.
I take shelter to evade the jerkish wind.
Shivering behind a measly tree stump,
no longer bold enough to admit
I think I'm in love
with nature's wit.

Longing Your Sweet Name

Genuine love written in your name,
for I hope as much the same
before the scorching hostile summer
wilts the vitality of life, and aflame
sand dunes shift their shape in eternal snowy slumber.

Lingering thoughts of admiration
sing in praise; oh, I hear the birds
sing in praise as you waltz in the wind
among this solemn place.

Muse by the nature of your gaze,
rich ruby-red, fluffy petals—exquisite form!
Oh, how you amaze today
and swarm to amuse the neighbors
with a ravishing smile on your face,
from beloved scent that bolsters their devotion
to the jocund wave in their travel on this day.

I am enthralled by the sheer expanse of your aura;
I am ashamed I have not bloomed to pay homage.
I have much to flourish from my juvenile state,
yet there you are without judgment.
Nourish me each morning, awash by the radiant light
that surrounds you daily,
thus I am complimented greatly.

Loving You

I often wonder in the pleasure
and nature of a kiss
whether I should bother to treasure
everything in this woman's kiss.
For a time, I trace and measure what I miss
as distance is unkind to give view,
and allow the mind to reminisce;
for someone like me thinks of loving you.

A damsel alone in her room,
she often dreams, me and her, clutch in silken hands;
from that scene, something beautiful blooms:
We stroll across silver sands,
and on this night, nothing demands
the union of these two,
where feelings spring and seize form—then imbue.
For someone like me thinks of loving you.

I often wonder in the pleasure
and nature of a kiss
whether I should bother to treasure
everything in this woman's kiss.
For a time, I trace and measure what I miss
as distance is unkind to give view,
and allow the mind to reminisce;
for someone like me thinks of loving you.

Sometimes, sweet moments meet themselves in the abyss;
sometimes, darkness passes through
and enters places to dismiss,
for someone like me thinks of loving you.

Motion

Love grants the motion
and teaches lovers how it's done:
Bundle up emotions,
muster all you can before it's all gone.
Love distills the sweet and spice.
lovers never knew how twice
the mind is encased in ice,
betting the lovers in a roll of dice.

Love shames the lovers to ride it out,
as every move ain't the same.
Must scour within and pull out
the very thing that held seduction's name.
Ah, yes—once absorbed in temptation,
lovers begin the experimentation.
Where minds implode,
each microsecond, finger-shadows
dance another round before they explode
and wake the next day in the meadow.

Here's one, below the chest,
while the other rubs the breast.
This pristine state of sweat has shown
no quarrels and permits the lovers' rest,
for this motion has flown
one's hunger for more;
one's hunger will bore
one's vigor evermore.

Ode to Love

I

We scour lonely for a time to press together the rift
between one soul and another under the dreary tides
of life. Noon marks the labor we tithe in spirit
to relinquish the joys of glancing eyes, kindling
the blithe youth. The enmeshing of two dancers
working their way to harmonize in rhythm,
toiling in endless practice until they finally meet
at the summit of two—conjoined as one union,
inflamed by the fire of passion giving form
by the taboo only love can offer and amalgamate as one.

II

The frolics of youth changed with autumn;
devoured by the faceless, frigid, scorned shadow
of the subtle beast, the fragility
hidden in the cave and family came through
as our spark in the night and we learned
what nakedness revealed, that of our mortality
in the company of loved ones. We have grown together
as compatriots to battle the beaten battered nature
of unyielding paths, bolstering the love of those
surrounding, fermenting a future together to no bounds.

III

We plug away between the dings of devices;
the likes to each of their own fill a drop in our well-
being, the twenty-four-seven propaganda of divides,
the triviality of coffee stains in our Benz; meanwhile,
we do these things in the matter of living. We could
find in our haven the hobby that stirs the soldiers
to charge into war with the sheath of their swords,
and over that laborious hill we are awestruck to find
the revelation of hymns that urges us to sing! As
the journey of the craft leaves us feeling wholesome.

IV

The journey is strewn with many forks
in the road, as some are more taken and
as some are quite vacant, hidden among the shrubs;
thus, we learn from the sanctity of wisdom
there are those behind where our worth has their value.

V

The gift of life wasn't the gift of life itself,
but the gift of love by the Logos themselves.
Bestowed with the magic to love and be loved
has made all the difference to transcend and
connect the trinity of love as one with all.

Reminisce

Reminisce in the expression of a kiss…
Dazed, sunburned forearm; *is this not bliss?*
Remiss not to admit
in the expression of joined lips…
Meet better ends, drip
in a state—extinguish by a class of flame
from former years of life;
how those former years of selfsame
did not in kind held the bliss of strife.

Mi Amor,
allow bonds to endure as arcane legends:
a mural on walls conveyed like Egyptian hieroglyphs.
A romanticized tale of two plain people
with tempest-swept pasts,
united under the constellation of stars,
foretold millenniums, adapted and altered in movie slides,
paying homage to lovers' sublunary tides.

The magic gleamed in those eyes…
envisage an unswerving allegiance that thrashes;
long ago, abide by darkness strife,
shattering to upend the life of lies
and all struggles subside from the flutter of her dark lashes…

Illuminated journeys farther to arrive—
one will discover in wisdom conviction that transcends.
A transparent gem mingled in a sea of sand,
how the view in those shimmer-eyes has shown faith;
cadence has never wavered in her speech,
and the way her lavender scent obviates dire wretched wraiths.

Ponder the grace of her form
and how some vagrants once were are no more.

Unlike her, a steadfast desire to curb the psychosis
bubbling beneath the surface.
Oh, how wondrously she elevated from a stained history
and ascended the peak to uncover the endearment of love.
Against all those odds, despite all those adversities,
how does one not adore the prosperity of her efforts
as she lent her one-wing cavalier seraph her comfort?

Sex

Sacred form of bond unleashed;
from its chain sparked a temptation so

endless; each second of the moment
coursed through my veins with an addiction so
intense my heart convulsed in rampant fury.
The struggle escalated to jerk my body
in disjointed manners,
I felt a rise in temperature as the heat
settled in every artery,
A friction swelled before a scene to

exhibit; should I go further? Further in this steamy
drenched place
with marks carved like cave paintings.
What lay ahead? Pleasure's grim face
should probably be buried in a treasure chest; so
as we lay in it to rest and drift away like sand in the hot air.

Silhouette of Love

The day I set eyes on her,
an arrow darted my feet and did not set apart.
A shadow glanced over; my body cringed and sneered,
as I feared.

As she spoke, words seemed vague—
was she God's work or the Devil's dreadful plague?
I had overstayed my place
but needed to know what would become of this play.

She leaned over and pressed into me;
overwhelmed, I leapt back to skim what it meant.
She clutched herself into my arms to anew a world of charm.

Then our lips locked—
a sensational bearing aroused in fantasies;
snow had taken form, and it was clearly reality.

Thinking of You

I often think of you.
The image us going astray
provokes the fear of loss of you,
drives me to yearn for a magical way
to rid my concerns; my dear loving grace,
I found on this unearthly dreadful place.

A naive love, better than a life of doubts,
could not crumble when lies are told about.
Shall we bolster what remains of our whereabouts?
Shall we foster what ordains us as beloved spouses?

To admire everything about you,
the kind gestures demonstrated in language
sent from the stars to guide under the dark blue
and protect along the cobbled road of anguish;
unknowns ahead and rewards in short supply
cannot unwind the endearing love of goodbyes.

Sew hearts together as one gleeful union,
and sup the sweet nectar that has proven
the company of two cannot depart
from living a fairytale with a joyous part
that agrees to role-play in such imagination
than a reality of decadent dissolution.

When I gaze at the moon, I hear a tune—
a song I made—so I take it and sing it to you.
I await to see in those eyes what swells to elate
and create a life that mates to procreate
and share with the world that we're soulmates.

Despite what life has put me through,
I recite the moments of breakthroughs,
oh—on this night as we lay in bed,

what excites me is how the fate of threads
could not clip with their shears
the years
dwelt in that place,
thinking of you—I've longed to face.

True Love

A word of love in vain—
how did I sustain such pain?
Bold as I may be, I still hold the memories of agony.
Reminisce in my mind, to find a fresh fable of you
that lingers throughout precious time.
Form an angel from above,
dorm in the roots of cupid's love.
The purity of your heart
imparts me with the security of encouraging love.

HEARTBREAK

A Great Loss I

The one I love vanished without a trace,
banished beyond this realm.
I am in a state of distress,
unsure how to bear forth and face
the warmth at my bedside misplaced,
never knowing when the shattered glass will ever get replaced.
No one
must know of this; she is
Gone.
At first, they would sympathize,
then involve the police;
they drowned me with questions,
not long from now, they will mark me as a suspect,
in no time, they will exercise my rights;
soon I'll feel the neighbors' menacing eyes;
it will drag me into further depression,
the onset impression
gone from their faces.
I cannot alarm others with this grim situation—
in good intentions it's best to let go, and
not involve others. Let them envision my action
with suspicion.
I'll do what's right,
I'll search the heavy moss,
I'll endure the savanna smoldering welt.
I can't seem to put aside the loss,
Why the hell did she not tell me how she felt!
She lay at my bedside—but why?
While this dread hangs over me—I wish it to die;

should I ruminate her kittenish face?
But the house has a hollow space.
My mind is torn,
I wish this dread had never been born.
Charon, here is a coin; ferry us into the void
and do not allow my atoms to reanimate
for another poor soul is jaded with my troubled soul.
Cast me into the sea to float on an endless drift, so
I'll shift into slumber and
never wake from this tumble sea-drift.
I'm fading away; who will console my soul?
Where does the heart depart?
A raised question, but no one imparts an answer;
I slouch to lay my head into eternal rest,
my spirit wandering into the nocturnal forest;
can you take up my request to replenish my form
before the storm sets in?
The leaf changes hue in September,
temperature lowers in October,
leaves brown in November,
and temperature plummets in December;
this will be a long, long winter.
They often cite seasons as a sign of hope, but
much into Spring, the ground is still buried in snow
for reasons unknown;
scientists baffled by the phenomenon,
theologians shouting Armageddon;
drifting in my blanket snow mound cover,
a few words, humming along as the icy winter takes over.

A Great Loss II

It is time to wake from my slumber,
covered in my snow mound shelter.
But it brings so much comfort—why should I bother
when the world is blanketed in frozen water?
I toss and turn; aghast the adjacent bedside
is bitter and bleak,
and not a trace of her seen for weeks.
And my palms retreat to a weak face—
What a fool I am to think she'll unfold at my side today.

A visceral sensation boils, akin to suspecting someone
in the wee hours, and yet
it gnaws incessant for hours;
I toss and turn to shake it off,
not long until it returns to agitate;
I tell it to knock it off; an unyielding persistence,
I wish to distance—made its claim to aggravate.

Her kittenish face, clawing for attention,
rubs the flake from the dry salt-laden ice.
Dark and warm in my snow mound cover;
yet, why bother?
Lifeless the world is…
Aimless the heart is...
How nice to not think twice
about leaving my snow mound cover...

Then, I bend upward and punch away the cover!
A cool breeze glides in and shivers;
I prop up half my body and gaze around
from my snow mound.

A time-lapse stillness, shown in its kindness,
preservation of things, in her likeness,
I hop out and hurry about,

scanning around for a route that will lead the way.
Off I go into the blissful wilderness,
and the jester of clime leads me astray.
I trek into the obscure beating snowfall
and wonder how long a marathon would be my downfall.
Yet, I end nowhere all the same.

Alas, the unforgiven chill of the selfsame
does not chase and let on with its resounding fears,
but gives notice to a sounding screech, piercing my ears,
the hem in wool-like texture, ruffling in the icy-wind,
takes shape as I adjust my gaze
and trace the silhouette of my lady's grace.
As clarity yields to reality, a fixed visage
propels a pressure from neck up to my face,
fish-eyes proliferates with a void,
a reflection shown with a force that destroys
the tides of doubts that fester upon the iron gates of life!
And yet, strife recedes by the
gentle tousle of arms to my sides.
Something destined fills this place;
undestined to collapse into her embrace—
yet that I dreamt, that I dreamt,
which I pine, which I pine,
That I. That I. That I brace
this illusory chase—did not face
what would ever be mine...so
why bother and wake from slumber
in this warm comfort
in my snow mound cover?
Adrift, a few words hum along
while the icy winter falls over forever long.

A Lost Soul Mate

Once she stormed out the door,
the walls molded with sores;
as he gaped at the back of her head,
she never returned a mutual gaze.
An onset paralysis no longer holds,
a rift in his heart grows
the farther she goes—
a wedge lodged in his soul.

Stoic, he assumed more frightened than a newborn.
A generous love filled his inner being;
it knew no bounds, yet it was fleeting,
indiscriminate of secrets, written in their thesis.
Several hours had passed and he clenched his chest,
throat tightened, contraction in his face lengthened,
wrinkled eyelids refused to let go,
face glowing red like a hot iron,
eyes swelling larger than a man's lustful desire,
tears of loneliness made their escape, one after another,
and soon he wept, gloom filling the air all around four corners,
cracks bleeding in these walls of mourners.

Now he dwells in his cave, staring high at the ceiling.
Every song on the radio, sad one after another.
He doesn't know whether to go mad
and check-in with the asylum;
a buzz in his ears rings forever, a room
smothering in dead silence;
he overhears ants chatting with a look of pity,
his mind wanders to find a decent memory
to restore the hope he needs to get off his rocking,
creaking chair.
He musters enough energy to show a little self-care—
so comforting is the rocking, creaking chair,

the conservation of energy; why would he dare?
Prying eyes at his window are quite confused,
and he wonders, *how can I continue with this abuse?*
He wishes to get on his knees,
request in prayer, and plea
for a God to forbid his treacherous torture,
but he finds comfort within his maddening borders.

A love that once penetrated all the angst he had for life
now has desecrated the trust he has for life.
Calm and distraught,
what an unnerving paradigm he cannot escape,
unlike what he had hoped: a sound life with smoother rides,
only resulting in battering tides.
He thanked God every night for sending an angel;
now he wishes to ask the angel
of death, Azrael, an early request:
Could there be any sanctum,
so light can guide the way
and remove him from this dreadful place?
In such sanctum, he'll spend his days
repenting for forgiveness,
so it gives someone a renewed life,
who does not share in his illness,
his unquenchable lust for desire,
now gone in a smoke of fire.
He may not deserve to love anyone,
but let his lesson become wisdom to spare someone.
Maybe the aches will go away,
as he counts his days,
confident he will trust again
that he may never espy pain.
Soon she'll meet the one,
then her mornings will be spent at her lover's side,
glancing at the sunrise.

One day he slogs out the door;
Lady Muse's warmth rubs his face
to glimpse the morning sunrise.
She apprises him and he roams to find out more
and stands at the corner of a sidewalk,
whisked away in a breeze
as the crowd nears the end of their crosswalk,
off the coastline it goes,
into the vast ocean, it seems to know,
and a rumbling volcano knocks it off course,
farther and farther it goes,
a sun-drenched sailor,
smacked in the face
by a traveling bystander,
soon landing on an indigenous landscape,
rain falling in gentle taps,
then he coalesces.
A gaze resting across the bridge
stands a ridge
between two lovers;
as they utter,
a turbulent wind spirals in a vortex,
hauls away a couple lost soulmates.

Anticipation

Down in the dumps,
catching the blues,
what must I do,
to renew myself unto you?
In spirit and in mind,
a love distant and blind,
a clashing of lustful traits,
a heart smoldered in a clouded state,
where are you to comfort and soothe,
while fear and ignorance corrupt this fool?
Inability to carve out the memories
for all the treacheries
imbedded in overloaded sensory,
betrays me endlessly.
Doubts surmount,
whispering in my head,
I'm a fool,
I'm a fool,
I'm a fool!
These voices fill me with dread.
Where is my sweet chariot?
Don't delay the encroaching tides;
I don't think I'll make it by night's end,
because written in these lines
are the anticipations to be at your side.

Distant

When we part,
hearts begin to split apart;
if it were a nightmare
with a beast's long stare,
a feast it would have with my arm.
So much of this childish harm
cannot be thwarted;
no heavenly body shields us from uncertainty.
Where a spotlight once was, a beacon led distorted
bodies to fade into dotted darkness.
Souls embodied into hellish landscapes.
I can't tell from where it came, nor how it got its name;
no matter how far away,
the Caspian Sea is quite blackened on this bizarre day!
I hope to furnish a bridge that once led thee—
when the day should arrive, nourishment
will spring from a tree
and supple the next of kin in a delighted glee
and cement how
distant apart
happened in an instant.

From Your Valentine

From your Valentine
all those trysts weaved in time;
a farewell to thine.

Worlds apart, I knew you were mine
as beloved lavender followed wartime—
From your Valentine.

Hazel eyes lucent as the stars' shine
did not lie on this cloudless clime;
a farewell to thine.

The dew wedged between two lips, combined;
lost in limbo until the ringing of chime—
From your Valentine.

A smile to upend the imminent strife that pines
the fire in men, until then, this verse's rhyme—
a farewell to thine.

At the charge with my lavender vine,
and by night's end
relinquish by divine's prime;
From your Valentine,
a farewell to thine.

I Miss You I

I miss you as time skips,
while I trip over it.

I miss you when the streams rush,
while I stroll the park
thinking of you very much.
I miss your touch when we held hands—
I frowned and bled when you
left behind into the dreadful land.

The moon glows when you're near,
then it dims as I fear.

I long to hear your sweet voice;
as it is clear you were meant to be here.
I miss you, dear; it has been years
since our lips wedged a kiss.
What my heart desires most is this.

I Miss You II

I miss you as time skips,
while I trip over it.

I miss you when my heart misses its pulse,
while I stroll the park
thinking of you very much.
I miss the warmth when we held hands.
I frown when you're not here,
but off in the badlands.

My moon glows when you're near,
then it dims as I fear.

I long to hear your stories;
nothing more than a series
that fills me with joy.
As it is clear to me you're meant to be here,
let us indulge all those years
that brought two lovers
before dying embers.
I miss you, dear; it has been so many years.
I miss you more than the river that flows beneath my feet,
and I pray before our hairs grow gray that we'll meet.
I am glad you're blessed with kindness in those eyes;
because of you, I will languish and wait
before the night dies.

I Miss You III

I miss you as time skips,
while I trip over it.
I miss you when my heart takes its rush,
while I stroll the park
thinking of you very much.
I miss the sensual feeling
when we held hands.
I am met with an unsettling
omen,
ringing in my head;
you're nowhere to be found in this shadowland.
My moon glows with luminosity when you're near,
then it dims as I fear.
I long to hear your soothing voice—
was it clear I made a good choice?
I miss you so, dear;
now I'm lonely, engulfed in fear.
I miss the percussion of your kiss,
like a concussion that held my heart in bliss.
please, return my lover
before my love dwells eternal in the abyss.
Love's tide flows stronger,
toward absent lovers,
in the abyss.

If You Were Here

If you were here,
would you feel my warm embrace?
Could you conceal micro-expressions on your face,
when the air of my fingers descends your back,
and then ascends back up your neck
and trembles in place, wondering in flashbacks
if I misplaced, leaving you feeling like a wreck?

If you were here,
would you hear the deep rural poetry that swept vales
and echoed through wheat fields brushed by gales
then reached the peak of the inmost gorge by the outskirts,
comforting and flirting you to fall asleep?
Every night tortured by the memories
that lingered throughout the frosty nights
as you wept on countless nights—scour to find joy
in the most lonely of times.
If it was not for Costard's l'envoy,
I could have my shares of my lady's salve to enjoy;
ruminate from the vacant room and favor
in hope for us to become whole as the nights waver.

If you were here,
when eyes cross, you would coy;
shy to look with those conceited eyes,
I glance away; you yearn to spy,
then my swift eye meets with your glisten-eye-speck—
it takes my heart by surprise, I did not expect.
Firing within our cells,
a complicated chemistry unwrapped our clothes and we fall
on the bed of fame—exposed by the fascination of our bodies,
we chuckle in shame, insecure by our flaws,
and sweeping our thoughts, we find perfection in union.

If you were here,
the night would await a chapter in our story
and tonight's call shall compile our history.
I shall hear your plea and ghostly pass through these walls,
spread the bud of your rose, intertwined between our souls.
A beam alights as it shoulders from the scene of a dream
and draws forth the magic of a gleam.
Seduce in pensive massages and kisses,
and fold her lips and press onto mine without glitches.
Pride has awakened from the zenith of heaven;
I strike the first blow—you shiver and growl and moan.
I feel proud—you ask for more and fall in a state of flow;
awash and overwhelmed, you quiver and dissolve like foam.

The moment lasted for centuries on seamless nights.
On the last day, I reminisce about the sweet pleasure,
adore in her smile as she lay there facing the window as treasure,
glinting in the sun and staring long at the wheat fields basked in light.

The enchantment of this morning seals the measure of our day.
My love daydreams: Two seeds of grain plough into the soil,
and sprinkle by jovial clouds
and twinkle of the Milky Way endows,
spawns the seeds that ameliorate
heavy sighs blown from breath,
sprouting sprightly heads to overcome Death.

Love Document

It has been so long since last you rested your palms,
five years since.
The sun doesn't shine in these qualms
for that reason:
I've plucked up a pen and pad,
and written off this pain,
unknowing of how long it will sustain,
and all those memories with it drifted away.
The unforgiving tick-tock makes no room for feeble souls.
And so not a day flies by that I do not sob,
as a man bears his bravery in a world with no swab,
wearing his misery on his sleeve;
unable to hide the melancholy
that wrings his heart, and in their leave
they're all swift to shame masculinity.

Sometimes, we believe loved ones can ease the burden,
but what is the worth
when words can't describe in dearth?
And what happened to guardian angels?
They use to shoulder our sorrows;
are we naive to judge the grandeur above,
responsible for all life's tasks? Does
the ball of light anchored in the sky
shelter love with vitality and dye
half our days from our inner-demons who spy?
Once rooted, now a burial spot for precious dreams;
what bribery cajoles these sorrows for fruitless labor,
a symbol etched in elaborate patterns.
We hold our breaths, unable to decipher, and belabor
our minds to the point that they shatter.

The situation is much more severe than what's
begged of us to discover our resolve,

but we missed the mark and did not learn
how valuable our patrons asked of us to solve.
Even though the law of physics
and the holy scriptures can't save the metaphysics
of pains which we wish to cease,
they wish an epoch of peace
in the blissfulness of youth,
never inflicting a wound
so the soul remains intact in a sigh of relief.
But as language lives, all words are drawn in blood and found
the earth soaks its nutrition from the flesh that Mother
bore and bores new flesh given to a tired hand,
sets down its pen and cradles his Father,
and asks if love can save a man from his insanity
before this reality welcomes the devil inside of me.

Missing Note I

A musical note chiming along,
emphasizing the percussion of a song.
Once a heart steady and bold,
nowadays has fallen weary and cold;
she consumed herself in the haze,
then, *poof*—evaporated in the blaze.
My legs had roamed until gray grew in a moment of days.
A horror unlike others shows in my face,
a sign of her remains unaware;
days and nights become a nightmarish flare.
As the missing note stretches on,
my heart will linger, thinking if this was ever our song.

Missing Note II

A musical note,
worn and torn something I once wrote,
long ago, I once knew
a melody I composed,
a forgotten milestone.
As I watched, she erupted in flames,
amazed by the sheer audacity.
A string was plucked from my guitar,
and a long pause in my song drove me to paint.
Days and nights, I thought it was bizarre—
she would leave a bridge in these notes
with too much pause.
Now I write with veracity,
but nothing is coming along.
I tuck away my instruments,
and what is left is written on
this musical note:
"I bid you a farewell song."

No More

I collapsed when you hustled out the door—
perhaps giving up will spare you from the worst.

So many stages of aggravation,
our frustration boiled over and reached its climax.
No more to unveil, this juncture showed
what moved behind the curtains
and revealed the wounds we concealed in canisters.

All marks will manifest to diverge us on divided roads,
now all afoul; no more joy to relish
but an unwavering torture looms in remembrance.

We locked up the heart behind a nailed door;
bones faded to ashes
and all those slithering mouth games we played
perished;
jubilant thoughts deprecated as jagged dust grains
carried and blew into the bitter bleak winter;
as the onlooker peeked behind the rearview mirror,
intentions vanished in the blizzard.

Love's glow dimmed.
May Lady Fate have her purpose for severing us—
I found a love,
I could not show its stains,
and actions could not state the pain
of reincarnating as a symbol of hope;
I suppose it's true—the sole thing we could achieve
was accept no more…

Prosper Love

Disarray for all the pressure I'd impart,
fret not for the pressed pain sheltered in your heart.
Dim light did not reach the couple's alcove,
but a trove of secrets laid and wished to consecrate
the devil's unfettered nature.
But spirits deserve better—
we've witnessed depraved trials, scene by scene, and yet,
innocence still deserves better,
and we vowed what tethered us wouldn't ever sever,
but sever it did.
Whether we served what's best for healthy lovers
I won't ever know of this,
as terrors manifested and devoured our efforts.

Tried to put the past behind to reclaim our health,
but it caught up before the next breath,
all sealed up in flashbacks still haunting us to death.
I cannot willfully blink it away
and I beg of you to stay;
I'm unable to change my nescient ways,
bombarded with random states of outburst only to stumble,
and how could someone who absorbs all those blows live humble?

I reflect on the season of May;
it unmasks your better nature
as the promise of sunlight stretches
the bud of flowers to shake off droplets of morning dew
and gives rise to a renewed hope; yet, too
soon these months descend in their darker nature—
careless, repulsive, pensive malice—
as the heart's inner wounds seem beat,
but an inner glow reveals a passion so grand
that makes the elites
tremble in their castle peak…

So, I ask not the month of May,
but may the seconds hasten their intentions;
while the dawdling minutes cloud the mind each hour apart,
sever the tides that once balanced my heart.
I reminisce from my perch
and dwell from that once sacred affection
and observe the trembling of an aged soul
caught in an affliction.
Fogged memories are no wiser when the full moon
tacked on the night sky loses its glow
that once filled my whole room.

I shudder and roll in bed awaiting the sunrise,
a forlorn setting that will never arrive,
and yet I wonder if love will prosper
from sea to mountain, from earth to heaven,
as the night persisting in the eternal twisting void
gives form to a gentle, bitter darkness raven.

Shallow Love I

There stood the innocence of light,
where childhood memories
came unto me as dreams of the night—
as I stand at the edge of a precipice,
ought not love is certain
or ought hope for other than pain
was the genesis and exodus of my plight.

Wherever I'd tread,
I ended back where I stood.
So many times have I done it—
Built up to bombard without impedance, but
patience is quite virtuous.
There are those to trust
and those who poke with their pitchforks;
for how long will the torment excavate my heart
and dismantle the best parts?

A symbol representative of true essence
left its mark as it faded from adolescence
and still received no rejoice out of my convictions—
my words seeped filth,
actions went unrecognized,
so, I made a proposition
for all the wickedness
born from my thoughts.
Maybe for once
I should remain
a manifestation of nothingness.
Where before,
love was a lantern in the dark,
now it is a fear lodged in my soul
near the dim celestial sphere of sorrow.

Shallow Love II

A child indulged in his imagination,
embraced his childhood hero's personification.
A memory he took in vain
as love went on and astray,
as a hopeless illusion of instrumental pain.

He would have surveyed his soul
but his shadow was faint and motionless,
tormented as time orchestrated,
living by a false virtue,
yielded a fool.

It clawed at the poor child's spirit
and left him a symbolic impression
as his essence diminished by adolescence.
He chose not to acknowledge,
convicted by his acts of selfishness,
forming an evil composed of wickedness.

Maybe for once, he shall now remain
a manifestation of nothingness;
where before, love ignited a lantern,
guiding him through the dark,
now fear swells his heart
in the bleak, barren void, devoid of a spark.

Unconditional Love

My life is yet another plague
for saddened souls—we sound so vague.

My eyes, my lips, my ears, my nose, a descendant discrete,
the shadow severs the aspect of Being in me;
yet, it idles; my heart idles in retreat.

Celestial Being, redeem my wounds as my love results
confounded in another Shakespearean theme.

Fool me once it will come; fool me twice it has been done.
Shame on you to ever think I'm the one;
shame on me to ever believe in love.

You and I were never meant—
that is why unconditional love is a myth.

LOVE OF LIFE

A Distance From You

No matter the distance, a thousand miles apart,
no matter the walls,
love draws me nearer to my sweetheart;
in any moment death calls,
a risk worth the adventure.

I'd trek the scorching Sahara Desert,
stumble through the harshest of winters;
a feverish cold or ash-fingertips won't stall where I need to go.

No matter the distance, a thousand miles apart,
no matter the walls,
love draws me nearer to my sweetheart;
in any moment death calls,
a risk worth the adventure.

I observed from an Amazon treetop canopy
a citrus scent making its course and gently
signaled a fatal attraction; rife with danger—
yielded a temptation of abundant lust, salivated a thirst,
devoured a ripe fruit as the sunlight gleam hung off it too.

No matter the distance, a thousand miles apart,
no matter the walls,
love draws me nearer to my sweetheart;
in any moment death calls,
a risk worth the adventure.

I await the day I can percolate my fingers down
the Waipio Valley.
The natives poked me one too many times to mar my skin;
but no matter how far you are,

a cage cannot hold as I pry the bars—
out I come in a lion's roar, eager for blood,
mopping the floor to reach my prey
before the blossom of my flower bud.

No matter the distance, a thousand miles apart,
no matter the walls,
love draws me nearer to my sweetheart;
in any moment death calls,
a risk worth the adventure.

Soaring the high heavens battered in the tumultuous
journey,
shouting out a sigh of relief,
teardrops of anticipation drew me nearer to await a soothing melody,
and an incessant thirst filled my mouth and advised onward the journey.

No matter the distance, a thousand miles apart,
no matter the walls,
love draws me nearer to my sweetheart;
in any moment, death calls,
a risk worth the adventure.

I had much to swim, swim among the seven seas,
and an ill-feeling grew within the belly of the beast;
chugging seawater to stay afloat, afloat the seven seas
and distance so vast—I tired;
I pressed on to accept my consequence;
and conditions grew dire.

No matter the distance, I shall sling my body across the stars,
navigate as sailors did, star by star,
and reach the solar system that holds my sweetheart.
I'll discover a route as I topple over planets;
with each breath,
I inhale toxic fumes; with each breath,
I restrain to save what is left in my suit,
for I made a promise to at least gaze at the lining
on my muse's face.

No matter the distance, a thousand miles apart,
no matter the walls,
love draws me nearer to my sweetheart;
in any moment death calls,
a risk worth the adventure.

I'd crawl on hands and knees;
I'd shuffle across lava pits lit in ashes on my feet;
I'd tip-toe over a swarm of tarantulas
in the Puerto Rican jungle
while their fangs tried to drill into my feet;
I'd paddle my way through a turbulent river,
bashed between weathered and battered rocks, but—

No matter the distance, a thousand miles apart,
no matter the walls,
love draws me nearer to my sweetheart;
in any moment death calls,
a risk worth the adventure.

Nearing the end,
I'd wrestle a bear and wind up with several scars,
clothes ripped apart from the grizzly beast;
yet, it has not killed me.
I'd climb from mountain crest
to mountain peak regardless of their hest,
frostbitten by the time I descend and four seasons
have passed
and did command—I will join her one last time, but—

No matter the distance,
what has fallen before has not broken me
from closing in a thousand miles apart.
No matter the walls,
love draws me nearer to my sweetheart;
in any moment death calls,
a risk worth the adventure
I'll do a thousand lives over,
no matter the venture.

Days of Our Lives

Today is much the same as yesterday,
as yesterday is much the same as today,
and tomorrow very much like yesterday and today;
an uninterrupted roll of film
lends itself a familiar bland from one
into the next without interruption and thrills;
much of the same wind blows east
from west; west it goes into the long, distant east,
it curls and clashes to form the beast,
swallowing its own tail, the unrelenting serpent,
ouroboros, done with purpose to cement
the cycle of life and death.

I pause—aghast! If words not set the mind on fire,
I tire with my pen before it grows dire;
Oh, fair day—wondrous, benign day;
do the seraphs of heaven undergo
the wax and wane of night and day
and contemplate with palms on elbow and chin, and say,
        "What a gift yesterday and today
            observed in the praise of psalms?"
I pass upon a star to secure a locket;
should an accident befall?
At least they will find my gratitude in this vow;
should chance not call,
death will not halt us and beat out life's aspect it ploughs.

Oh! Have you known the unknown
measure of care family can show?
No, unlike unhappy families a happy family
do show some measure of care in their own way.

Countless days,
when Lady Muse fires me with unrelenting creativity.

Countless days,
I rub my brow, staring at a blinking vertical line, endlessly.
The ease of words that flow with each click-clack on the keys,
bubbling from the chambers of Mount Vesuvius,
quite analogous to the barometers of daily life.

Months are long, months are short,
don't they ever, to the beholder, seem enough?
Perhaps, I prove the lot of us are actors on display.
How well the performance of actors' play,
rousing the applause of spectators to act another day.

I soften my mind and ruminate how
the ideas in our labyrinthine minds; holding greater truths,
dissipating with time, for life and its irregularity
makes no compromise
and the sublime cruelty of reality
invites the impulse to hide the wise
soul that knows how to arise
from idle hands and allows the boons
of life give note that strife
will not steal the best of loved ones.

Thus, let tingles of youth saturate the nerves
and spark an unwavering warmness in our hearts,
and we rejoice, as days of our lives, should they have served.

Maiden's Myth

The familiar spoils of joy dawn themselves every morn.
On the hillside ridge in the Fjord did born
late noon to roll in the coastal sands, and carved dunes
and stroll upward the grasslands under the blood moon.

The thrill did bore the joyous departure laid ahead,
and said: *Viva la Vida*; extoll the flames that bred
journeys unveiled the Warrior of Light; in spite,
the Warrior of Night availed its aim of blight.

Only something amiss held the key to my heart—
a star shot across a cryptic message to impart,
a secret only I could unlock, did not heed;
yet, enticed by a gnaw, and urged—venture with speed.

Hidden, only this night could reveal in the Fjord's bypass.
I stumbled upon a temple and entered its sole pass,
a peculiar charm in its atmosphere of August
etched in the walls in glamorous tales: a divine goddess.

Archaic letters littered about, shrouded in mystery.
If only I could decipher glyphs behind this beauty,
for it filled me with wonder and limitless awe.
Perturb by these halls with no end in sight, I dared not thaw.

Yet did I understand? The thrill of this adventure
billowed the moonlit crimson tides to censure
the strife I denied from my life; but joy had sprung
the further I ventured, and this venture I swung.

Something at the end captured me in trembles—
the room alighted, four torches helped center its vessel,
and there she stood, having aged well in her slumber;
what mirrors unveiled the maiden's myths from under.

Sweetest Thing I know

The rebirth of Spring flowers' bloom
no longer must I adore from my room.
Energy packed in Spring's passion
draws seekers of love in fashion.
The sweetest thing I know
spreads its wings at this time of year.
Cordial company comes and goes
and always nobly present to hear.
The striking balance of gentle breeze
met with the warm ambient sun.
Love's meaning blossoms in the trees
when Springtime's youth has spun
and shown the occasion in May,
satiating lovers' embraces each day
is the sweetest thing I know
and what scares me most:
a world upended to find and know
a silent deep ocean filled with ghosts
of creeping predators unlike any sort;
surface, shallow waters of dim souls
dragged beneath the depths of grim, dead sea scrolls.
Oh—the deep, dark ocean, sinking
while the tides smother unflinching.
Awaiting is a nocturnal beast
right underneath my feet,
and with those menacing eyes,
it sickles the soul into pieces,
and I'd be wise
to stay away from beaches.
I think it's best until next time
we meet in heaven's slumber in the frothy rime
of a cave-dwelling in the abyss,
away from the waning shaft of soul's kiss.

A day will compass come, oh—it will come
as the column of heaven's light pierces
into the void of hell's fierce forces.
So that light's hopeful allure will take form,
and tickle the hide of darkness strife;
and storms will waver and invite
the season of Spring
and bring the sweetest thing I know of life.

Power of Love

Honeymoon Bliss

Impermanence of life lowered its wings
from the ignorance of jocund good days;
strayed us from the most important of things
in people we love and adore, but slay
by all the obstacles of time, did bore
the willful blindness that upends and shoved
out the wonder and miracle of yore.
The toy has lost its gleeful charm and proved
trivial to passing aggressors; we
did not see the change in our temperate;
beneath the silt lay lies the deep, dark sea,
and finds in nakedness the shame of chaste.
Thus, vow hearts of hearts, no boundary holds,
nor no mountain, nor no couple to mold.

Love I

Oh, love does not examine the authenticity of its claim
nor fear in the presence of its aim;
just as bitter love wishes neither to proclaim
nor burden souls with rambling quarrels of triviality.
Oh, love beloved in music's melody,
course every meal, refine in savory matrimony.

Love is undeniable as it yearns to nurture
life's goodwill forthright;
bitter love is deniable as it craves to nurture
its own spotlight,
reassure to a God-given spirit let us bolster our defenses
should it ever falter our senses,
then heaven's gate shall anchor Ariadne's thread
and guide us to reach our homestead.

Love made its way in hearts to furnish like wishing stars;
love holds no grudge, but remarks the pain branded in scars,
in time subsiding in the next celestial sphere.
Love has shown the cruelty in this world,
steeped in their castles for all to hear:
Persecuting the masses with their diabolical sophistry,
stirring the passion of revolt in our hearts
much grander than the sum of its parts;
from collective will, we unite and keep our souls chapped.
Love draws forth the power to cleanse our poison-minds
and fall into the arms of our brothers and sisters in kind.

Love, I raise no claim to doubt your aim;
please do not sham as I oft indulge in pleasures.
Love, I see no beauty in imaginary figures;
troubled by the knowledge of abstract language
scowl faces of those entangled in paralanguage.

Oh, love does not examine the authenticity of its claim
nor fear in the presence of its aim;
just as bitter love wishes neither to proclaim
nor burden souls with rambling quarrels of triviality.
Oh, love beloved in music's melody,
course every meal, refine in savory matrimony.

Oh, love,
elevating warm touch, ashes bones to iron-corpse.
Oh, love,
amalgamate the molting feel of your presence in mine
and replenish the bland hue that marred in marks.

Love endures as time animates
the subtle creep of wrinkles,
and flowers wither and stars lose their twinkle.
Love's timeless and guileless
essence over eons of passing winters
remains selfsame as the universe ever grows
darker, colder, further.

Love does not reason alone but consults the council of two;
love does not treason but pulses with time. Is it not true?
Love does not demand words with the crazy few.

Oh, love,
you have shown me how your existence
grounds me.

Oh, love,
how you eviscerate the strife
that aspires to permeate one's life.

Oh, love,
ferment in solace, love and hate
an ever-enigmatic duality.

Oh, love does not examine the authenticity of its claim
nor fear in the presence of its aim;
just as bitter love wishes neither to proclaim
nor burden souls with rambling quarrels of triviality.
Oh, love beloved in music's melody,
course every meal, refine in savory matrimony.

Love, you are more than skin deep,
and the search in your chasm shall reap
to find the pure, pleasant myth laid in cryptic glyphs.
When the chosen can see the gifts
of love's divine form,
vanquishes the nihilism that plagues us no more.

Love II

Not a moot point to address
when I conceptualize love:
Beholden, is it like its largesse?
Smitten! You trickle me to rove.

Will you heed my plea of love's theory?
And help me marry a story,
a far cry of horrid chapters?
Writers, dare not invite readers.

I search in the elusive dandy's methods;
I search in the wisdom of Nicomachean Ethics;
I search in the data collected;
I search in the moralist eclectic;
I search in senescent couples' devotion;
I search in the phrases of renowned poets;
I search in the nooks of tree lines;
I search in dreams that weren't kind.

In my search to uncover love's beacon,
in those many nights of beaten
chills that I bore under many
blankets, hoping to kindle any
warmth in these tireless snowy
stilled seasons,
I could not work out within reason
as the wind bashed these hollow walls
and chilled a hearty place that called
for love to furnish at the hearth.

Mistake love for lust,
unlike in moderation, it busts!
Desire in youth's foolishness
would twist the truth and bleed a hollow soul;
Oh—time courses and happiness
seems much further from its glow!

Love, not in youth can they yield you!
A balmy resolve is not yielded by fools!

Love, the involuntary action of virtue
held in courage that nurtures us too.

Love, bitter lovers rise to oppose your treacherous deeds;
in their afterlife,
they latch onto the hem of your skirt to be freed!

Love, I cannot complain of the imperfect, sweet, somber bell
that jingles weary thoughts of perfect tells.

Love, your fruitful and elusive nature
can gift students the essential knowledge
that bears the prudent polish
of an emotion that glows and masquerades as divine;
what hovers in the shadows are the victims
who were most vulnerable to your crimes.

Love is Prudent, yet Vague

Winters, where love is held warm.
Summers, where we seal our love in the cozy dorm.

Another fable whistled in the wind,
erased in gods' confined temples,
a manuscript, true in its content and form,
now throughout the ages of monstrous storms,
shall perish as stone to dust and more.

Time, consumed or cherished,
remains arcane to the beholder,
for as love is a pretense of history,
the incense of its lust fills the void in human hearts.

Love another pretext of trivial matter;
where it once stood concrete, now fallen in idle chatter.

Love's Paradox

If love were of no crime,
then love were of no time,
as fond feelings often yield
and devils attempt to steal.
Incite—a chain of events
one cannot escape dull sense:
How to think, how to act,
we shrink from the fact
that we are zombies with a single aim
one cannot shake.
Unable to shake;
unable to escape;
unable to evade;
unable to discern;
unable to reclaim
one's reasonable aim, in
one's faculty of concern.

Temptation

I yearn for the temptation of my wife
to mourn, deny, and give rise to new life.
I shall start and descend from the region
of olives' nectar breast cries out demons,
gently pass my way in the scorched, steamy
sands of the flesh-eating belly of
Threshold guardians, and shout, "I'd journey
hell's desolate valley, and land
among a place unexplored by men and
advise an audience." Permission granted
by the authoritative stare in those eyes.
I know not to deceive, I've only had
one chance, it cannot afford to go bad.
As one to the other, lift and unclothe,
vacant skies hold two distant stars pledged in troth.
In one kiss, stoke the flames of desire
with each holy touch flown to admire
the friction of two souls wedged at limbs,
and evoke static discharge between skins
in the praise of ecstasy that pins
a cascade of bodies as they sing of hymns.

The sight of a kittenish visage
turns my breath skittish;
oh, cruel, untamed beauty cannot bear
with coarse hands nor alter in fair
the clashes of two forces swirling upward
and blown between breast utter by the Word—
deafen, the pounding that robs me of pride;
soften, within the heart, pledges to my bride.

Each second pulses in shivers
to awash and sweep down the flaming river.
A skyless night reveals the ire of the moon,

stirs the tides to lift and swirl into maddening typhoons,
smashes against the land in equal cascades;
unfurled, the everglades hide within its shade.
The steadfast land swings wide
at the brow of an angel in disguise;
the tides recede as the moonlight dims—
I know not but rekindle the dying cinder
that burns its soft yellow hue and tinder
the ritual of kings who brim
in protest their ruins,
whose wanton a goddess's flowering thorn,
whose famine starves and scorns;
if no thrall will dance in flawless
blows but glows in haste of feverish August.

The shadows of souls dance in the fire
and mourn a room devoid of light;
further under the full moonlight,
in the moot frost nips waning in December,
a banshee screech echoes in silence, "Remember."
And the speaker replies, "Time is unkind to match
the fantasy in latter-half of ages to love's ember."

The Color of Love

Lonely hanging in despair,
tied up at the end of twine,
a noose snapped and untwined,
dispersed in air;
not a soul in view to show their care—
yanked upward and incapacitated by the divine!
Do eyes deceive? Rub them once more
to find a glow exude a mortal form.
Wings so vast they blot out the sky;
matching the stain of a silver swan,
a halo hung over high
at the break of dawn;
originated from heaven.

The heed of a former prayer
lay a bridge between sin and moral character.
Eras lost at the hands of human nature,
the demise of it all, fell to its downfall;
a vertigo effect reverberated in the soul;
graceful hands seized mid-fall and the ire of hell's inferno.

Summon the spirit to help reach the ledge—
there stood an angel silhouette at the edge.
A brash, childish love did not falter;
before rest, laid at the bedside altar
and beseeched forgiveness to one's depraved vanity
soured the machinery of humanity;
could this angel save me from amnesty?

Hollow seasons were disorienting—
the mortality of our times alone
could aid the perception of truth
in the morbid habits we succumbed to.
Instill the humility to uncurl

the essence of inner-wisdom;
help grow when instances of life's lies
are utterly hopeless.

Aid and free the bramble
that enclosed the heart
when faith stood solitary in pain
but soothed by divine arms,
saved the last thread of faith and
preamble the heart's return to its sacred haven.
And wave above where you ascend heavenward,
and hope for the dying world that souls see
the color of love in thee.

EPILOGUE

Twilight

Eons—eons ago, celestial bodies
mingled uniformly
in the great sunder of the cosmos;
second to the singularity,
given form of day and night, an utmost
design by the hands of the divine;
fundamental elements would rise
from the nascent navel and subtle
collapse of mass fomented the painful
union; a dark, dreary catastrophe
of coalesced celestial bodies.
Clashed and carved, organs smelt of red-iron;
eons—eons past, cooled in tranquil-relief,
the void no longer spans the coupling of two
from the monumental history that bore two.

Pass the brink of dawn; among the meadow and lea
ruminate on a long, long, lost, sacred time;
before the spite in men's heart couldn't see
the lust for conquest tainting their war crimes;
but soothe by your nightfall grace,
but move by my daylight praise—
contemplate, contemplate, does your mind fixate?
When our union ever becomes eternally whole,
when your time is present, I dream to locate
imaginary curves held firmament on heaven's pole;
bridge a staircase by those sweet lips
my lips have not kissed, quite since.

Hang the solitary moon with spectacles of light—
recompense dormant lovers with the subtle might,

soothe the savage in men's thorny hearts with my touch;
lament how your absence would ever humble this much.
Fantasize, fantasize how the mind fixates
and recount a time that forever held our union,
and wonder in your presence the nuclear breath that blew
those to traverse the unknown plains that create
the collective unconsciousness that ignites humans'
passion to push pass their hubris boundaries; if they knew
the passion that stirred the miasma we once were,
perhaps the love of one's devices would remain a blur.

Each passing sunset, each passing sunrise,
occasion the union of dawn and dusk.
Meet and mingle at the hour of twilight;
from this ephemeral period, we share stories
of earthly species, of most rational lifeforms
who struggle with the paradox of their twin-form,
ravishing in turmoil o'er political reform;
each lunar ascent, each lunar descent,
occasion the union of dawn and dusk.
Meet and mingle at the hour of twilight;
ball of fire ascends from the underworld
from the vantage of two, where worlds meet.
Ball of glow fades in the veil of shadow
from the vantage of two in their retreat.
Two celestial bodies are not lonesome wanderers,
conjoined in the brief-history of uniformity;
two embodiments of spirits reside in
the majestic abode of heaven.

Please Review This Book!

Reviews help authors more than you might think but also readers; it will help spread the word by reaching more readers who can glean value from this book and pass it on.
If you enjoyed *The Cool and Warmth of Hearts*, please consider leaving a review—it would be greatly appreciated—truly.

JASantana.me/ReviewCoolHearts

Free Audiobook

DOWNLOAD THE FREE AUDIOBOOKS!

Grab your FREE audiobooks of *Shadows Amongst the Threads* and *The Cool and Warmth of Hearts*, narrated by me!
Experience the chilling world of fear and the passionate realm of love in a whole new way.

JASantana.me/ShadowsHeartsAudio

DOWNLOAD THE FREE AUDIOBOOKS!

Grab your <u>FREE</u> audiobooks of
Shadows Amongst the Threads and
The Cool and Warmth of Hearts, narrated by me!

Experience the chilling world of fear and the
passionate realm of love in a whole new way.

JASantana.me/ShadowsHeartsAudio

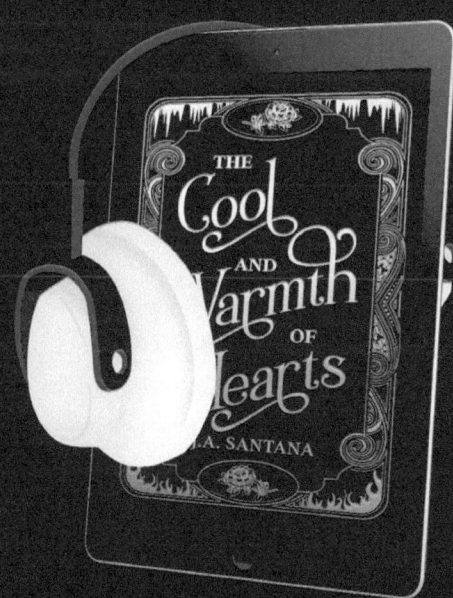

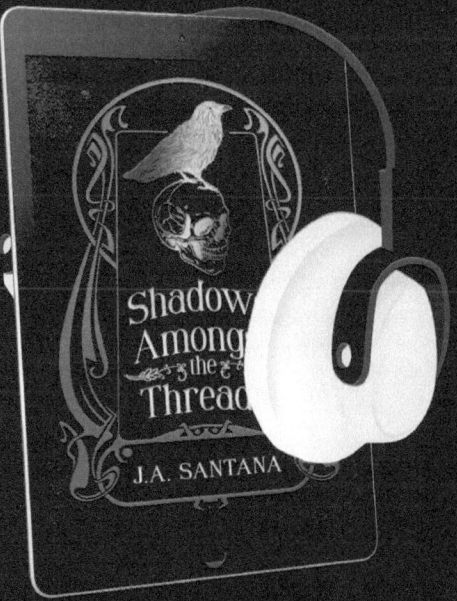

ABOUT THE AUTHOR

Driven by a passion for writing, Jose seeks greater wisdom to impart through his work. He craves new experiences, seeking to delight readers by transporting them to imaginative places through his writing.

He believes in using his stories to gain a deeper understanding of human nature and the human condition—including both the good and the bad within us. Jose is particularly interested in exploring the meaning of life, death, and what may exist beyond our realm. He aims specifically to discover insights to help people better navigate the world and the journey of life.

He draws inspiration from diverse sources such as mythology, history, psychology, philosophy, science, and his own keen observations. In *The Cool and Warmth of Hearts*, Jose examines the timeless facets of romantic love, from pining and passion to heartbreak and healing, offering insights that resonate with the universal journey of life and love.

Connect with Jose

jasantana.me

YouTube.com/@jasantana

jasantana.me/socials

More books coming soon.
You can sign up to get a sneak peek of the books I'm writing, notified of new releases, books I'm reading and recommend, giveaways and pre-release specials.

Acknowledgements

There are so many to thank and acknowledge who have influenced, inspired, mentored and/or supported me, this section would be quite longer than the actual book. With that said, I will do the best to make this thorough and concise.

Thank you to my parents, Francis, Agnes, and Jose Sr.; brother Andy; my child Tsunade; our cats Nature and Vincent; Uncles Juan, Alberto, Alex, Willy; Aunts Camille, Denise; my cousins Frankie & Erica, Will & Amanda, Jae & Crystal, Jessenia & Danny, Alexandra, and their children. Thank you to the rest of my family and those no longer with us (I miss you very much: grandpa, great-grandpa & great-grandma, Alexandra, and Blacky and Fluffy). Thank you to my closest friends Steve and Latonya. Thank you to the mother of my child, Linda, and her family. Thank you to the many friends and acquaintances I've known and gotten to know on my journey. Thank you to the artists, poets, authors, psychologists, philosophers, and to any that I miss. Thank you to nature and its splendors and thank you to the logos itself.

Thank you to my editor Michael Martin and my book cover & typeset designer Natalia Junqueira for their patience and professionalism in my book collaboration process.

Thank you, reader, for giving this book a chance and hope for the added value it has on your life, and it continues to do so as some source of wisdom and contemplation around the nuances of the shadow.

Thank you, writing community, for the invaluable wealth of knowledge in the production and marketing of a book; especially the overwhelming amount of information to run an author business.

www.ingramcontent.com/pod-product-compliance
Lightning Source LLC
Chambersburg PA
CBHW020413130626
46549CB00006B/2547

9798985462012